A CHEMICAL NIGHTMARE
BALD EAGLE COMEBACK

BY TIM COOKE
ILLUSTRATED BY EDU COLL

BEARPORT
PUBLISHING

Minneapolis, Minnesota

BEAR CLAW

Credits: 20, © FloridaStock/Shutterstock; 21, © Laura Hedien/Shutterstock; 22t, © guentermanaus/ Shutterstock; 22b, © Edwin Verin/Shutterstock.

Editor: Sarah Eason
Proofreader: Harriet McGregor
Designers: Jessica Moon and Steve Mead
Picture Researcher: Rachel Blount

DISCLAIMER: This graphic story is a dramatization based on true events. It is intended to give the reader a sense of the narrative rather than a presentation of actual details as they occurred.

Library of Congress Cataloging-in-Publication Data

Names: Cooke, Tim, 1961- author. | Coll, Edu, 1996- illustrator.
Title: A chemical nightmare : bald eagle comeback / by Tim Cooke ;
    illustrated by Edu Coll.
Description: Bear claw books. | Minneapolis, Minnesota : Bearport
    Publishing Company, [2022] | Series: Saving animals from the brink |
    Includes bibliographical references and index.
Identifiers: LCCN 2021002686 (print) | LCCN 2021002687 (ebook) | ISBN
    9781636910451 (library binding) | ISBN 9781636910529 (paperback) | ISBN
    9781636910598 (ebook)
Subjects: LCSH: Broley, Charles 1879-1959. |
    Ornithologists--Canada--Biography--Juvenile literature. |
    Ornithologists--United States--Biography--Juvenile literature. | Bald
    eagle--Juvenile literature. | Bald eagle--Canada--Juvenile literature. |
    Bald eagle--United States--Juvenile literature. | Eagles--Juvenile
    literature. | Endangered species--Juvenile literature.
Classification: LCC QL696.F32 C663 2022 (print) | LCC QL696.F32 (ebook) |
    DDC 598.092 [B]--dc23
LC record available at https://lccn.loc.gov/2021002686
LC ebook record available at https://lccn.loc.gov/2021002687

For more information, write to Bearport Publishing, 5357 Penn Avenue South, Minneapolis, MN 55419. Printed in the United States of America.

CONTENTS

CHAPTER 1

THE EAGLE MAN'S DISCOVERY

During the 1940s, Charles Broley became known as the Eagle Man. He was a bird lover who studied bald eagles in the United States and Canada.

LOOKS LIKE THIS PAIR BUILT THEIR NEST NEARLY 80 FEET* UP!

*24.4 m

Charles climbed the tall trees where bald eagles nest to **band** young birds. These bands helped **identify** the animals so Charles and others could learn more about them.

Over several years, Charles banded more than 1,200 birds.

THERE YOU GO, LITTLE FELLA.

Charles discovered that bald eagles fly north during the summer and south in the winter.

Charles also kept track of how many young bald eagles he found each year. In 1946, he found 150 birds.

One year later, Charles noticed a dramatic change.

THAT'S ONLY 80 YOUNG EAGLES THIS YEAR!

WHAT'S GOING ON? WHAT COULD BE HAPPENING TO THESE AMAZING BIRDS?

CHAPTER 2

A SOARING PAST

Bald eagles have a long history in North America. In the 1600s, there were as many as half a million bald eagles living throughout the **continent**.

Many communities respected and admired bald eagles for their speed and hunting skill.

After the United States became a nation, Americans continued to honor the animal. The bald eagle became a **symbol** of freedom.

How did things become so bad for the bird?

When **pioneers** moved across America in the 1700s, they cut down trees to build houses, towns, and farms.

Cutting down so many trees reduced the size of the eagle's **habitat**.

THWACK!

The birds had fewer places to live.

A lot of people hunted eagles as well. They were afraid the birds would attack their **livestock**.

BANG!

Over the next 200 years, many bald eagles were killed, and their population steadily grew smaller.

11

By the 1940s, so many eagles had been killed that President Roosevelt signed a new law to protect them.

But their numbers were still falling. Charles wanted to find out why.

CHAPTER 3

SAVING THE EAGLES

Charles asked researchers about the pesticide.

COULD DDT BE HARMING BALD EAGLES?

IT'S POSSIBLE. LET ME LOOK INTO IT.

Researchers discovered that Charles was right about DDT. The pesticide was first used to keep insects away from crops.

But the DDT got into bald eagles through the food they ate. The chemical was very harmful to the birds.

DDT took away **calcium** from the eagles' bodies. Without it, eagles started laying eggs with weaker shells.

The eggs broke easily, and many baby eagles died.

Charles worked hard to spread the news about how DDT was hurting bald eagles.

DDT Danger to Eagles!

BAN DDT

DDT

BAN DDT

Soon, others joined in the effort to save the eagles and to stop the use of the pesticide.

To help people learn more, Charles often gave talks about these amazing birds. He was even the first person to take a color film showing an eagle feeding its babies.

Charles died in 1959 at the age of 80. But his efforts to save the eagles lived on.

The use of DDT slowed down for many years, and in 1972, the chemical was finally **banned**.

The ban was very helpful for bald eagles. Just 10 years after Charles's discovery, the bird population had doubled.

Other people continued the hard work to learn more about eagles and keep them safe from further harm.

Today, more than 71,000 **breeding** pairs spend **mating** season in the lower 48 states. These amazing birds were saved from the brink.

BALD EAGLE FACTS

In 1973, Congress passed the **Endangered Species** Act. This law protects animals and plants that are in danger of dying out. Activities such as hunting, capturing, harming, or collecting endangered species are illegal under this law.

The bald eagle was one of the first animals listed under the Endangered Species Act. It helped them come back.

BALD EAGLES HAVE A WINGSPAN OF 6–8 FT (1.8–2.4 M). THEY ARE ABOUT 30–36 INCHES (76–91 CM) LONG FROM NOSE TO TAIL.

BALD EAGLES EAT MAINLY FISH FROM LAKES AND RIVERS. THEY ALSO EAT RABBITS, SQUIRRELS, BIRDS, SNAKES, AND DUCKS.

The bald eagle population in North America was between 250,000 and 500,000 in the 1600s. The population today is estimated to include more than 300,000 birds.

OTHER EAGLES IN DANGER

The bald eagle is one kind of eagle that is making a comeback. Other types of eagles are also struggling.

HARPY EAGLE

The harpy eagle is the largest kind of eagle. Harpy eagles are very rare, but no one knows how many there are. They live mainly in the South American countries of Guyana, Venezuela, and Panama. Breeding programs are helping these eagles make a comeback.

THE CLAWS OF A HARPY EAGLE ARE AS BIG AS A BEAR'S CLAWS.

PHILIPPINE EAGLE

The Philippine eagle is the second largest of all eagles. These birds live in the Philippines. There are fewer than 500 left in the wild. That makes them one of the rarest birds in the world. Breeding programs are working to save these birds.

THE PHILIPPINE EAGLE IS THE NATIONAL BIRD OF THE PHILIPPINES.

GLOSSARY

band to attach a ring to a bird's leg to help identify it

banned not allowed

breeding producing young

calcium something in teeth, bones, and shells that makes these things hard and strong

continent one of the world's seven large land masses

DDT a poisonous chemical used to kill insects on crops

endangered species a group of animals in danger of dying out

habitat where a plant or animal normally lives

identify to tell who someone is or what something is

livestock farm animals

mating coming together to produce young

pesticide a poisonous chemical used to kill insects and other pests

pioneers the first people to live in a new area

symbol a thing that stands for something larger than itself

INDEX

READ MORE

Harts, Shannon. *20 Fun Facts about Bald Eagles (Fun Fact File: North American Animals)*. New York: Gareth Stevens Publishing, 2021.

Kenney, Karen Latchana. *Saving the Bald Eagle (Great Animal Comebacks)*. Minneapolis: Jump!, Inc., 2019.

Khalid, Jinnow. *The Bald Eagle: Our National Emblem (America's Favorite Symbols)*. New York: PowerKids Press, 2021.

LEARN MORE ONLINE

1. Go to **www.factsurfer.com**

2. Enter **"Eagle Comeback"** into the search box.

3. Click on the cover of this book to see a list of websites.